How to Get Bookkeeping Clients Quickly

The Bookkeeping Business Marketing Guidebook

by Sylvia Jaumann

How to Get Bookkeeping Clients Quickly
The Bookkeeping Business Marketing Guidebook
By Sylvia Jaumann

Almost all freelance bookkeepers struggle with the issue of getting bookkeeping clients at one time or another. This book will give you more than thirty ideas for promoting your bookkeeping business even if you have a low or non-existent advertising budget.

"I am happy to say that since I have acquired your 'How to get Bookkeeping Clients Quickly,' I haven't had to spend so much time researching marketing strategies, writing sales letters, creating mailing lists formats, spreadsheets as well as how to write press releases and ad's for my business.

Furthermore, I had the hardest time trying to figure out how to write a résumé for my business as well as the vision and mission statements. This helped out quite a bit. Your pre-written letters have saved me a lot of time. It was worth the money, in my opinion.

Again, thank you!"

Candice Thompson
www.BlankCanvasBookkeepingServices.com

"The information is absolutely fantastic and dead easy to follow for all walks of life that are interested in gaining new or additional bookkeeping clients. This is a must have package, especially for small bookkeeping businesses as it's very difficult to obtain this quality of information anywhere!

I thoroughly recommend this package without hesitation to anyone who is after professional and exciting ideas to either kickstart their bookkeeping business or to help their existing business flourish with new clients ready and eager to jump on board."

Jason Lynch

This publication is designed to provide accurate and authoritative information in regard to the subject matter covered. It is sold with the understanding that the publisher is not engaged in rendering legal, accounting, or other professional services. If legal advice or other expert assistance is required, the services of a competent professional person should be sought.

First Printing, 2010

ISBN: 097388794X

Printed in the United States of America

Dedication

This book is dedicated to the freelance bookkeepers
from all over the world who contact me daily

Contents

"Work is either fun or drudgery.
It depends on your attitude. I like fun."

Colleen C. Barrett

Introduction

I know from personal experience that the hardest part about starting a bookkeeping business is actually lining up clients. For many bookkeepers, this process takes a long time and can be extremely frustrating.

The goal of this book is to help shorten this process so you can get bookkeeping clients much faster than if you attempted to find them on your own.

This follow-up book to *Secrets of Starting & Running Your Own Bookkeeping Business* was written to give you even more resources for promoting your bookkeeping business. *Secrets* was written to give you the fundamental start-up information and get you moving. It provided "the basics" when it comes to promoting your bookkeeping business, but this book takes you even further.

There is a great deal of promotional ideas in this book to get your phone ringing. Start off with a few and then gradually add others. Some methods may work better than others depending on your local market, so don't be afraid to experiment a little.

Your first step will be to establish a budget for your promotions. Some methods are free while others will cost you. Your best bet is to mix and match, using some paid and free methods. Not only will this save you money, but it will help to expose you to a wider audience.

Advertising is a large part of every business, but as a freelance bookkeeper the good news is that it's not a constant expense.

This is because after you've picked up a few clients you'll find that you won't have to do much advertising, as frequently new clients come through referrals from existing ones. Also, once you have all the clients you want, as long as you keep doing good work for them, you won't have to keep searching for new ones.

A large part of your promotional choices will be based on your personality. If you are a "people person" and enjoy chatting with new people, then you'll probably have no problem attending business functions and meeting people that you'll find there. However, if you tend to be shy, you may find you prefer more "hands off" types of promotions such as placing newspaper ads and writing sales letters.

Whatever you do, don't let this process overwhelm you to the point where you don't get anything done. Just take it one step at a time. Set up a schedule and write down which promotional method you plan to do; then do it. Hold yourself accountable.

After all, the biggest challenge when it comes to working at home is staying motivated and getting the work done.

So let's get going!

Chapter 1: Getting Started

"The reward for work well done is the opportunity to do more."

Jonas Salk

Creating Your Advertising Campaign

To get started, I recommend you create an Advertising Campaign spreadsheet, which is essentially a plan to help forecast your advertising budget.

Advertising your bookkeeping business is a process that is done over months. For best results you need to diversify and run a multifaceted Advertising Campaign that uses several different marketing methods.

Your potential clients need to see your advertising message between five to seven times before you can expect to see results. Experts say that 81 percent of major sales are closed after the fifth advertising contact. This means that you have to use an assortment of marketing methods to expose potential clients to your bookkeeping services in order to see results.

For the best coverage, it's important to promote your bookkeeping business using both offline and online methods. That way you cast a wider net and your message is more likely to be seen.

Start by developing an Advertising Campaign covering a period of at least the next three months. It will probably take more time than you initially thought to get clients, so be prepared with enough start-up capital to keep you going until then. If you can, start part-time and keep your full-time job until you start to pick up clients. Then you can slowly transition into full-time bookkeeping.

Plan your advertising budget and break it down choosing a variety of advertising media. Do not skimp on your budget.

Although starting a bookkeeping business is a less expensive business to set up than other businesses, you still have to invest enough money to make sure your message is seen by potential clients. So budgeting at least $250 per month is not unreasonable considering many other businesses spend upwards of thousands of dollars every month to promote their businesses.

Here's an example of what your Advertising Campaign spreadsheet might include:

	A	B	C	D	E	F
1				MONTHLY	# of	COST PER
2	ADVERTISING MEDIUM	DATE	COST	BUDGET	CLIENTS	CLIENT
3	**January**					
4	Sales Letter	01/17/10	75.00			
5	Press Release	01/15/10	100.00			
6	Display Ad	01/23/10	75.00			
7	Business Cards	01/31/10	50.00		2.00	
8			300.00	250.00		150.00
9						
10	**February**					
11	Web Hosting	02/04/10	10.00			
12	Display Ad	02/13/10	75.00			
13	Sales Letter	02/21/10	19.00			
14	Classifed Ad	02/27/10	50.00		2.00	
15			154.00	250.00		77.00
16	**March**					
17	Web Hosting	03/05/10	10.00			
18	Classified Ad	03/15/10	50.00			
19	Bookkeeping Association Fee	03/21/10	250.00			
20	Sales Letter	03/21/10	75.00		2.00	
21			385.00	250.00		192.50
22						
23	**April**					
24	Display Ad	04/03/10	75.00			
25	Sales Letter	04/15/10	19.00			
26	Classified Ad	04/18/10	50.00			
27	Web Hosting	04/23/10	10.00		2.00	
28			154.00	250.00		77.00
29						

Chapter 2: Promotional Tools

"Family, religion, friends... these are the three demons you must slay if you wish to succeed in business."

Monty Burns

A Word About Branding

Creating a "brand" for your bookkeeping business helps create a consistent image of your company.

According to Wikipedia:

"Consumers may look on branding as an important value added aspect of products or services, as it often serves to denote a certain attractive quality or characteristic. From the perspective of brand owners, branded products or services also command higher prices. Where two products resemble each other, but one of the products has no associated branding (such as a generic, store-branded product), people may often select the more expensive branded product on the basis of the quality of the brand or the reputation of the brand owner."

As you can see, branding is important not only because it adds a consistent quality to your marketing messages, but it may also allow you to command higher bookkeeping rates.

Branding, in a nutshell, consists of using the same colors, fonts, style, logo, and taglines throughout all your marketing messages. So make sure you keep this in mind as you develop your promotional strategy.

Business Cards

Networking is one of the freelance bookkeeper's most effective ways to get new business. But networking doesn't mean much if you don't have a good way to turn that initial contact into a second contact. Your business card is the tool you use to do exactly that.

Lots of bookkeepers look at business cards as an "old school" way of getting business. They don't think the cards are an important tool. So they'll slap together a card that includes the standard information, such as name and contact information. Big mistake.

Your card needs to accomplish a few goals:

1. It needs to look professional. In other words, it needs to leave the right impression.

2. It needs to give the reader your information at a glance. If the business owner digs up your card three months from now, will he or she know who you are and what you do? Your business card should make all of this information clear.

    For example, a card that says "Jane Doe Enterprises" doesn't help the reader at all. Putting "Jane Doe, Bookkeeper" is better. But including a title (bookkeeper) and a tagline is better still. For example, "Jane Doe, Bookkeeper. Saving your business time and money."

3. It needs to give the business owner a reason to contact you. A good tagline that conveys a benefit is a must. But you might also consider putting a coupon on the back of the card.

Your business card isn't just a listing of your contact information. Instead, it's a small ad for your bookkeeping services.

Here's how to create a good card that brings results:

Choose a High Quality Card

Don't skimp by choosing the cheapest paper. You want to use high-quality card stock that won't rip, tear, or fold easily (such as 100 lb premium paper). Plus, you want to use high-quality ink that won't fade or smear. Ask your printer to show you his or her full line of paper and ink options.

> **TIP:** Use a standard size for your cards. Some businesses choose to use oversized cards as a means of getting attention, but many people have standard-sized card holders. If you use an oversized card that doesn't fit into a holder, your card might not make it into the business owner's "save" pile.

Create a Readable Card

You don't want to shove so much information onto the face of the card that the person has a hard time reading it. You want the reader to be able to take in all the information at a quick glance.

One way to do this is by eliminating unnecessary details. It's common to put a fax number on a business card. But if you only receive a fax every once in a blue moon, just skip this information to help de-clutter your card.

Second, you should work with your business card designer to create font faces, font styles, and graphics that make the card attractive, professional, and easy to read. For example, using an "antique" font or a cursive font might look fancy, but it's usually hard to read. Or using a small font might give your card an edgy, high-tech feel, but that too is hard to read.

Give People a Reason to Contact You

As previously mentioned, you need a tag line or slogan that tells people what you can do for them. Here are a couple more examples of benefit-driven taglines:

- Your low-cost bookkeeping solution.
- A bookkeeping solution that makes dollars… and sense.
- Let me organize your books – professionally and quickly!
- Bookkeeping solutions that makes tax time a breeze.

The second way to get people to call you is by putting a coupon or other incentive on the back of the card. For example, "Mention coupon code XYZ to get 20 percent off your first month of services! Call me now at [number]."

Letterhead Stationery

The stationery that you use to send out your promotional sales letters doesn't have to be expensive. You don't need pricey linen grade paper. A decent quality regular paper stock is all you really need, especially when you're sending out large volumes of letters to potential clients.

If you like, you can buy two grades of paper, a cheaper one for mass mailings and a more expensive one for other correspondence.

> **TIP:** Being able to print your own stationery makes this a very simple procedure. Look for three sample letterheads (in Publisher format) provided here:
>
> **www.GetBookkeepingClients.com/gbc-resources.html**

Mailing Lists

In order to do your mailing campaigns, you'll need to put together a mailing list to send out your sales letters, newsletters, and postcards. This can be done a couple of different ways: by renting a list from a list broker or by creating one yourself.

Renting mailing lists of business owners can cost anywhere from $100 on up, and you can only use the names once. Look in your local Yellow Pages under "Advertising – Direct Mail." You can also do an online search for list brokers.

Alternatively you can develop a list for <u>free</u> by spending some time researching potential businesses in your local area. If you're starting out on a tight budget, I recommend taking this approach because the only thing it will cost you is your time.

You can put together this list using:

- Your local telephone book
- Chamber of Commerce member list
- City Hall business license directory

You may need to use a combination of all three to get all the information you require. You will need the following for your mailing list:

- Contact name
- Business name
- Address zip / Postal code
- Telephone number (if you plan to follow up with a phone call)

A	B	C	D	E	F	G
Contact Name	Business Name	Address	City	State/Province	Zip/Postal Code	Telephone

Bookkeeping Logo

Here's a quick and fun way to create a logo for your bookkeeping business (and it's free!):

Go to VistaPrint.com. Click on the "Free Products" link on the top left and select "Free Logo Design." Follow the prompts.

Here's a nice sample logo I created within a few minutes just by using this program:

FIRST RATE BOOKKEEPING

You can either save the logo to your computer or save it on VistaPrint and have them add it to your marketing materials.

Marketing Kit

Your bookkeeping business marketing kit is a professional package that you put together to showcase your bookkeeping business. It contains a:

- Biographical profile – which details your training and experience
- Company description -- a description of your business
- Vision statement -- what you strive to accomplish in your business
- Mission statement -- your goals for your business
- Fact sheet -- your list of bookkeeping services

This marketing kit can be mailed to potential clients or presented to them during their initial consultation. Having a marketing kit is not mandatory, but it will help establish a professional image in the eyes of potential clients.

Much of the information contained in the marketing kit will also be used on your bookkeeping website, which is why having this is not completely necessary. Also, the cost of preparing these kits can be expensive.

TIP: You'll find a sample of the **"Marketing Services"** kit here:

www.GetBookkeepingClients.com/gbc-resources.html

Chapter 3: Bookkeeping Website

The Internet is the most important single development in the history of human communication since the invention of call waiting.

Dave Barry

Your Website

Having a website to showcase your bookkeeping business is important in several ways:

- It's extremely cheap advertising (you just pay monthly web hosting fees after you've purchased your domain name and had your website created).

- You can post information on your services, rates, and other related bookkeeping information so that when potential customers call, most of their questions are already answered.

- Getting your website listed and linked onto local business directories is usually free.

Using WordPress

WordPress makes it incredibly simple to create your own website. This software is easy to use, provides a variety of templates, and offers excellent support.

There are many great reasons to choose WordPress to create your bookkeeping website. Features include spell check; previews; and autosave; the ability to post text, audio, and video files; a variety of privacy options; and the ability to track statistical data.

Some of these features may be more important to some freelancers than others so deciding whether or not WordPress is right for you will largely be a matter of personal preference.

Those who do opt to start their website with WordPress will certainly not be disappointed by the amount of time it takes to set it up. You can literally set up your website within a couple of hours.

This is tremendously important to bookkeepers who are eager to get started and do not want to deal with a long process to start a website.

The support offered by WordPress includes the ability to contact the support staff as well as the ability to receive support from other members through online forums.

Here are the basic pages your bookkeeping website should include:

Home Page

- This is your "welcome" page that offers highlights of your business and what it can do for the client
- You can list your phone number or email address here if you like
- You can include a photo (headshot) of yourself here

Services Page

- This is where you get to show your stuff
- List all your services here

Rates Page

- This page is optional and some people prefer not to use it (I personally believe it deters tire-kickers and time-wasters)
- List your hourly rates and state if you offer flat rates

Testimonials Page

- This page is optional as well but will really help to pre-sell you using the benefits of "social proof"
- You can use testimonials from clients or letters from employers here

About Us Page

- This is where you state all your education, training, certification, and experience
- You can provide some personal information but you should focus mainly on your business experience
- You should have a headshot of yourself here

Ecourse

Adding an opt-in sign-up section to your bookkeeping business website is a great way of getting bookkeeping clients while at the same time keeping your bookkeeping business foremost in their minds.

However, people typically won't sign up unless they receive a benefit in return. So one option is to offer an "ecourse" (or free report) to entice them to add their email and name to your sign-up form.

An ecourse is simply a series of articles on a specific topic that provides information to the reader. For example, you could do an ecourse on "why businesses need a bookkeeper."

TIP: You can purchase a "ready to go" ecourse that you simply have to copy and paste into your autoresponder. This nine-day ecourse was designed to help plant the idea of outsourcing bookkeeping in the minds of potential clients. In each lesson your subscriber will discover another compelling reason to hire a bookkeeper (i.e. you) while they overcome any common objections they may have.

Your bookkeeping business is featured prominently in each lesson, giving you free exposure for your business.

To learn more go here:

www.GetBookkeepingClients.com/enhanced.html

Using an Autoresponder

To successfully manage an email subscriber list, you'll need something known as an autoresponder. An autoresponder is a great asset to your website, as it can handle virtually any email you receive. You can think of these tools as salesmen who never get sick and are always there to answer emails twenty-four hours a day – seven days a week.

Autoresponders are very helpful tools that people can subscribe to. They can also capture and manage email databases collected from your website traffic. You simply use a sign-up form and capture both the name and email address for any of your website visitors.

You can add virtually anything you want to an autoresponder and send it out when you wish. You can also send out a broadcast message to everyone on your list at the same time, which will get your information out there and save you a lot of time.

I highly recommend you use **Aweber.com** as your autoresponder, as their deliverability rates are very high, ensuring that your email will get through to your subscribers and not get stuck in their spam folders.

Why Publish An Ezine?

After your subscriber has followed your ecourse (or read your free report), you need a way to continually remind them of your services without pitching them directly. A great way to do this is to provide a monthly ezine.

Not only can you achieve the benefits a conventional newsletter publisher enjoys without having to pay for mailing costs, you can easily and conveniently spread your influence and expertise to your base of subscribers.

The Three Best Ezine Formats

The text ezine is the most commonly published. The advantage of this format is that other than writing, you don't require any special skills to use a Word or Notepad program.

While the HTML ezine format requires a certain degree of HTML skills on your part, you can add more sophisticated features to your ezine issues, making them more appealing to your subscriber and thus increasing your readership value.

You can decorate your ezine format, change your fonts, include pictures, and more. However, the drawback often faced by HTML ezines is that they often get trapped into spam filters before they reach the subscribers' inboxes.

The third and least used among the three formats is the PDF ezine. Publishing your ezine in PDF format can consume a lot of time and effort on your part, but the benefit is that it's valued more and retained by the recipient.

> For a set of twelve ezines that will remind your potential clients about your bookkeeping services and is easily customizable, go here:
>
> **www.GetBookkeepingClients.com/enhanced.html**

Using Squidoo

Squidoo is a unique social site that allows its members to come aboard and build their own web page, which is called a lens. Members can build a lens on almost any topic so long as it isn't illegal. The best part is that it's free.

Lenses can be made as personal pages to connect with other people and share your details with them. They can also serve as marketing machines as Squidoo is a good way to get the word out about your bookkeeping business.

Building a lens on Squidoo is really easy with its step-by-step, build-a-lens interface. To create a lens of your own, all you have to do is follow the easy-to-use guide and enter details of what your lens will be about. Once you've entered your details, all it takes is a click of the mouse to publish your new web page.

The key to making this work is to set up your Squidoo lens using the keyword "your city" + "bookkeeping" (i.e. "Seattle bookkeeping.") Use this keyword term in your title, tags, and also mention it at least once in your content. This is so that your lens will end up near the top of Google (and that's what you want, right?)

If you have a website, make sure you link to it from your lens. If you don't have one, make sure you add your email contact information.

Once you have your lens created, you're free to fully customize your lens with videos, articles, visitor polls, and much more. Squidoo gives you the option to easily make your lens a cash generating machine, which is something that makes it unique among the many social sites online.

As a lens owner, you have an option to add advertisements from vendors such as Amazon to earn a commission on sales generated from your Squidoo lens.

The search engines tend to rank well-created, informative Squidoo lenses favorably in their search results, especially Google. This allows individuals to build lenses and get them in the search engine rankings fairly quickly. This is great for bookkeepers who can create lenses and point them toward their website.

There are Squidoo lenses for just about everything imaginable, from home business how-to lenses to gardening and model railroading. Just about anything you're interested in would make a great topic for those who share your enthusiasm.

If you haven't had the pleasure of creating a Squidoo lens, you're truly missing out on a really easy method to create a web presence in mere minutes. You will also be able to connect with others who share your interests and get traffic to your bookkeeping website—all with just a few clicks!

TIP: You can set up your Squidoo lens by going to:

www.squidoo.com

Chapter 4: Direct Mail

"Action is the foundational key to all success."

Pablo Picasso

Sales Letters

When it comes to planning your bookkeeping marketing strategy, it's no secret that sales letters should play a major part in your offline promotions. However, to be effective, a one-time mailing just won't cut it. You must mail out sales letters regularly to help reinforce your message.

Sending direct-response sales letters to business owners is a bit more expensive than some forms of advertising, but it can also result in a good return on investment. You only need a very small percentage of positive responses to profit or at least break even on your mailing costs. And once you factor in the lifetime value of a customer, you'll see a good ROI.

For example, let's say you send 500 letters at a cost of 70 cents per letter (postage and printing), for a total of $350. If you get just a 1 percent conversion rate, that's five new clients. Thus you can easily recoup your investment and make a profit on a small conversion percentage.

Here are some tips for creating a high-response sales letter:

Start Small and Test

Even if you have a potential mailing list in the thousands, don't send all your letters at once. Instead, create different versions of your letters (such as putting different headlines at the top) to see which one gives you the highest response. Once you've determined your "winner," then you can use that one for all future mailings.

Use AIDA

If you know something about writing sales letters, then perhaps you've heard about the "AIDA" formula, which stands for Attention, Interest, Desire, and Action. Here's how AIDA fits into a sales letter...

Attention: The headline on your letter is designed to grab attention, usually by presenting a big benefit or perhaps even by arousing curiosity.

Let me offer just a couple additional examples:

- "Let Me Take Care of Your Books... So You Can Take Care of Your Clients!"

- "If You Hate Business Paperwork, You're Going to Love This Bookkeeping Solution..."

Interest: The opener of your letter is designed to get your prospect interested in both your letter (so that he or she reads the whole thing) as well as your offer. You can do this by:

- Asking a qualifying question. Example: "Would you like a bookkeeping solution that saves you time and money?"

- Identifying with the prospect's pain. Example: "If you're like most business owners, you hate dealing with paperwork and you absolutely dread tax time..."

- Jumping right into the benefits. Example: "Finally, bookkeeping doesn't have to be a burden any longer!"

Desire: Here's where you make the prospect want to hire you. Typically, you do this by offering a list of benefits (usually in the form of a bulleted list) that tells the prospects what you can do for them.

For example:

- Full-service bookkeeping means you never again have to hire multiple people.

- Low-cost solution means you keep more money in your pocket.

- Makes tax time easy.

- X years of experience: If I can't organize your books and help you save money, no one can.

Action: Now that your prospect is interested in hiring you, your letter should close with a call to action. This is where you tell the prospect what to do next, such as calling. For best results, create a sense of urgency by using a deadline, such as an upcoming tax season deadline or a deadline to use a coupon.

Example: "Pick up the phone and dial [number] now to discuss your bookkeeping needs. But do it today, because I can only accept five new clients at this time."

Improve Your Response

Some letters will fall flat. You can help boost response by testing variations of your letter (as previously mentioned). Here are other ways to improve your conversion rate:

- Write like you speak. Picture your perfect prospect sitting across the table from you, and then imagine telling this person what you can do for him. You wouldn't talk like a rocket scientist, using big words and fancy jargon. Instead, you'd talk more like one friend to another. This is the same approach you should take with your sales letter.

- Orient your letter toward your reader. Your letter should be all about your prospect, his pain, and what you can do for him. That's because your prospects don't care about you. To that end, eliminate words like "I" as much as possible and replace them with "you" statements.

  Here's an example of re-orienting a sentence toward the reader. Instead of saying, "I offer a low-cost solution," try this: "You can take advantage of this low-cost solution."

- Include a P.S. at the end of your letter. That's because it's one of the most-read parts of a sales letter. Your

P.S. should reiterate a main benefit and/or restate the call to action.

- Send letters every month or so. You want to keep your name in front of your prospects. One way to do that is by sending letters regularly. You can send monthly letters to your warmest prospects (such as clients who've previously hired you for smaller, one-off jobs). And you can send letters every month or two to clients you're hoping to land.

- Follow up by phone. Most freelancers don't follow up via phone… so if you do it, it can help you stand out.

- Test a letter against a postcard. A postcard costs less but can be just as effective, especially since the recipient doesn't have to open anything. Most people will at least glance at a postcard since no extra effort is required.

- Get prospects to open your envelope. If you're using a letter, then you'll want to test variations of your envelope. This may include hand addressing the envelopes; sending envelopes that include your business name and logo; and putting a headline (benefit) on the envelope.

  This will take a little longer, but studies have shown that people are more likely to open a letter that doesn't look like "junk mail." Also, make sure that you use actual postage stamps and not a postage meter or indicia.

> **TIP**: If you need help writing sales letters, you'll find twelve sales letters in our "Enhanced Package" so you can send out one letter a month for an entire year. These letters are set up so all you have to do is merge them with your mailing list that you create using the Mailing List spreadsheet (also included in the package).
>
> Learn more here:
> **www.GetBookkeepingClients.com/enhanced.html**

Letters for Local Accountants

The most effective and least expensive way to get business is from referrals. By developing a relationship with the accountants in your area you will quickly be the first person the accountant calls when one of their clients needs help with their day to day bookkeeping.

Accountants are *always* looking for good bookkeepers to refer their clients to. It makes the accountant look good and saves them from an accounting nightmare at year-end.

Contact your local accounting firms to find out which accountant handles subcontracting and referrals for bookkeeping services.

Then write each accountant an individual letter introducing yourself and your company. Make sure you follow up with a phone call to arrange to meet with them. Some accountants may request a copy of your résumé detailing your work experience so make sure you have yours updated and ready to send along with a cover letter.

Make sure you follow up with individual accountants on a regular basis either by phoning them or by writing follow up letters. You may even want to invite them out for lunch so they can get to know you better.

On the following page is a sample of an introduction letter that you can use to send to accountants.

[Accountant's name]
[Accounting Firm]
[Address]
[Address]

Dear [Accountant's name],

Do you have clients who are in need of a good bookkeeper? As I'm sure you know all too well, having the books done properly throughout the year can save you a huge headache when you prepare your client's year end paperwork.

My name is [Name] and I run [Name of bookkeeping service] here in [City]. I have been a bookkeeper for [# of years] and have several references to verify my excellent bookkeeping abilities (see attached). [Attach copies of reference letters]

My bookkeeping services include:

- Payroll
- Accounts Receivable
- Accounts Payable
- Bank Reconciliations
- Government Remittances
- [Any other services]

If you have any clients whom you feel would benefit from my services, I'd appreciate it if you could refer them to me. I've attached a few business cards [attach 3-4 business cards] for you to pass out to clients whom you feel might benefit from my services.

I'll be calling you in a few days to follow up on this letter. I'll be happy to meet with you at your convenience to discuss this further.

Sincerely,

Postcards

Postcards are a relatively inexpensive way to send out a mailing with a brief reminder about your bookkeeping services.

Postcards can be made using software such as Microsoft Publisher and cutting a single sheet of cardstock into four postcards.

For the photo side of the postcard, you can:

- Design a colorful, eye-catching graphic
- Use a free graphic from online sources such as **www.sxc.hu**
- Provide a "question and answer" type design, such as:

Some clever businesses have even gone so far as to photograph the business they're targeting and use that picture on the postcard. You can guarantee that will get your postcard noticed! Although, clearly this is more work to produce, with the technology available today, it can be done.

> **TIP:** For samples of "Ask the Bookkeeping Pro" ads that you can use to create postcards, download them here:
>
> **www.GetBookkeepingClients.com/gbc-resources.html**

Chapter 5: Newspaper Advertising

"Advertisements contain the only truths to be
relied on in a newspaper.."

Thomas Jefferson

Newspaper Display Ads

While classified ads are confined to one section of the newspaper, display ads are the ones you see sprinkled in among the articles and editorials. They can be as small as a business card or as large as a one or two page spread. The question is: How do you use these ads to bring in fresh bookkeeping clients for you?

Choosing the Right Newspaper

The first step in starting a successful display ad campaign is to choose the right newspaper to advertise in. Because most businesses want local bookkeepers, your obvious first choice is to advertise in local newspapers. Later on you can expand to other cities and regions to attract a broader clientele.

Regardless of which newspapers you choose to advertise in, you must remember this—your ads must be placed where business owners are most likely to see them. A good choice is to put your ads in the "business services" section of your newspaper or in any business-related inserts.

TIP: Talk to the newspaper advertising representative to learn about additional advertising opportunities. For example, some newspapers put out special magazine-type business inserts once or twice per year. You'll want to get your ad in these inserts if your newspaper offers them.

Selecting Your Ad Size

The next step is to choose the size of your ad. While it's true that a full page ad gets more visibility, these ads are more expensive. Simply put, the return on investment might not be as good as a smaller ad. (But you may need to test this to be sure.)

As such, you should start with a smaller, less expensive ad: perhaps a 4" X 2" or a 4" X 4". You can then test this smaller ad against larger ad sizes to see which size gives you the best return on your investment.

> **TIP:** Some newspapers will measure the ad space according to the fraction of the page it takes up. In those cases, start with a small 1/16 or 1/8 of a page ad. The size, of course, depends on how big each page of the newspaper or insert is, so ask for the dimensions before purchasing ad space.

You don't have to pay full price for these ads. You can save money using these tips:

1. Negotiate. That's right, ad rates are open to negotiation. It doesn't hurt to ask for a lower price or other perks. This works especially well if you use the next tip...

2. Increase the frequency of your ad. If you agree to place an ad for several weeks or months in a row, you can usually get a lower rate.

3. Place an ad in multiple newspapers. Some companies own multiple newspapers in the same region. You can negotiate a lower rate if you place ads in their sister newspapers as well.

   When you're ready to expand your advertising reach, then you might consider using a service like http://www.usnewspapers.com/, which gives you a discount for advertising in multiple papers across the USA.

4. Ask about "remnants." This is a "stand by" ad that's placed at the last minute when a newspaper needs to fill space. You'll get a lower rate on these remnants.

Designing Your Ad

The next step is to design your ad. You don't want to use a solid block of text, as that's hard to read. Instead, use white space, graphics, and bigger fonts to draw attention to the ad.

Your ad will have two basic parts:

1. An attention-getting headline, which "speaks" to business owners. For example:

   - Business Books a Mess?
   - Attention Business Owners: Free Initial Bookkeeping Consultation
   - Make Your Tax Accountant Fall in Love With You

- Save Time and Money by Organizing Your Books
- Tax Time is Easy When You Keep Good Books

2. The body of the ad, which tells business owners why they should hire you (i.e., share the benefits of your service). The body should also include a call to action along with your contact information, such as a phone number and/or website. For example: "Call [number] now for a free consultation" or "Call [number] now to beat the tax season rush!"

Improving Your Conversion Rate

For best results, you need to run your ad regularly (preferably weekly). That's because business owners aren't constantly looking for bookkeepers. However, when a business owner does decide to hire a bookkeeper, you want your name to be the first one to spring to mind. And one way to do that is by running your ads regularly.

The second way to improve your conversion rate is to test your ads. That means testing headlines, ad bodies, your call to action, graphics, ad sizes, overall design, and where you place your ad. When you know which ads return the best conversion rate, then you can cut out the losers and focus on the winners.

You do this by "keying" your ad, which means you mark your ads so that they can be tracked. This is as easy as providing different phone numbers and web links in your ad. Or you may ask your callers or web visitors to provide a "promo code" for a percentage off your services. Either way, use different codes for different ads, and then track them to see which brings you the best response.

Newspaper Classified Ads

Another way you can advertise in a newspaper is by placing classified ads.

The downside of a classified ad is that it only appears in the classified section, which means fewer people will see it. The benefit, however, is that those who see it are highly targeted. That's because these prospects are actively searching for something to buy from the classifieds.

Here's how to run a successful classified ad campaign:

Place Your Ad Correctly

One of the keys to placing a successful classified ad is to choose the right newspaper. Just as with display ads, this often means starting with local newspapers since many business owners are looking for local bookkeepers, and then expanding out of your region as your ad budget permits.

> **TIP:** If there are any publications in your area geared specifically toward business owners, then you'll want to test your classified ads in these targeted publications.

Second, you want to place your ad in the right section to get the most exposure. Again, you're looking for classified ad sections that business owners are likely to read. Most newspapers have a "Business Services" section that should work well.

Choose Your Ad Size and Options

Here you're walking a line between good visibility and good value. You want an ad that's big enough to get attention… but you also want an ad that gives you a good return on your investment. For best results, you need to test different ad sizes to see which one is right for you.

For starters, however, choose a "medium ad" – not the largest and not the smallest, both in terms of size and price. You may choose certain options like bolding or outlining your ad to get more eyeballs looking at it. Check your newspaper or with your advertising representative to see which options are available.

> **TIP:** Just like other forms of newspaper advertising, the classified ad rates are open to negotiation. This is especially true if you agree to run an ad continuously for several weeks or months.

Create Your Ad

Your next step is to create your ad. Since you cannot use graphics in a classified ad, your ad needs to get attention through a strong, benefit-driven headline and an ad body with a call to action.

> **TIP:** See my notes on AIDA starting on page 40 for tips on writing good ads.

Since most classified ads tend to be small, you may consider using a two-step advertising system. That's because a small ad doesn't give you enough room to properly sell your bookkeeping service.

Here's how it works:

You place a classified ad with the goal of getting your prospects to step forward and identify themselves. Once they've done that, then you follow up with them to close the sale.

One way to do that is by offering a free, "no strings attached" consultation. This works well because it gets qualified prospects to call you. During the call you can upsell your paid service.

Another way to do it is by offering something like a free report that prospects need to request via email or postal mail, which gets prospects on your mailing list. For example, you might put out a report like, "Are You Making These Top Ten Small Business Bookkeeping Mistakes?" Naturally, the report should include a pitch for your paid service.

Test Your Ads

Just as with any other types of ads you place, you should be testing and tracking to see which ones give you the best results. You may find a direct-response ad in the business service section works best. Or you may find a two-step ad in another section works best. You won't know for sure until you test and track.

One final tip: People do business with those they know, like, and trust. Running your ads continuously helps build up that familiarity factor, which boosts your conversion rate. Using a two-step process also helps conversions, because it allows you to build a relationship with your prospects.

Chapter 6: Online Classifieds

"The remarkable social impact and economic success of the Internet is in many ways directly attributable to the architectural characteristics that were part of its design. The Internet was designed with no gatekeepers over new content or services."

Vinton Cerf

Using CraigsList

Savvy bookkeepers who market on Craigslist are able to gain a great deal of benefits by using this advertising option. Craigslist is an online community where users can exchange information, buy or sell items, seek jobs, or even find friends or romantic partners.

There are a number of benefits to advertising on Craigslist. Two of the most important benefits are the affordability and the ability to reach a large audience.

The Price is Right

Consider the cost of advertising on Craigslist versus advertising on other websites and there is simply no comparison. The vast majority of Craigslist postings are available free of charge to those who use the website.

Only a limited number of advertisements are charged a fee for posting advertisements.

Even these advertisers are only charged a nominal fee for their advertisements. This means all commercial advertisements for products and services are posted free of charge.

Reaching a Large Audience

In addition to affordability, another benefit to advertising on Craigslist is the potential to reach a large audience. Craigslist receives approximately twenty billion page views per month from approximately fifty million website visitors in the U.S. alone.

This is appealing because it allows users to reach a large audience with only minimal effort. Craigslist already has a huge following and many Internet users routinely turn to Craigslist for whatever they're looking for before searching other resources.

Having such a large audience means half of the work is already done for advertisers. They already have high traffic to the website; now they just need to write an eye catching and engaging advertisement that will attract customers.

Your Target Audience

Craigslist certainly has a large pre-existing fan base of regular users, but this large audience does not necessarily ensure advertisers will have a target audience just waiting for them to post their advertisement. Craigslist is an extensive online community and finding members of the target audience is more important than reaching the entire community.

Business owners can certainly invest a great deal of time and effort placing their advertisements throughout the different sections of the website, but this is not likely to be effective.

Craigslist is divided into a number of different sections and categories for a specific reason. This is to make it easier for users to find the information they're seeking. For this reason business owners should focus on placing their advertisement in sections that are likely to be visited by members of the target audience.

Additionally, placing advertisements in multiple sections may result in the moderators of Craigslist interpreting the advertisements as spam and deleting them.

How to Create Your Craigslist Ad

1. Go to the city which is closest to your hometown (scroll down by state / province)

2. Go to "Services – Financial" located in the middle of the page near the bottom

3. Click on "Post"

4. Choose the "Financial Services" category

5. Either log in to your account or apply for an account (they just ask for your email to do this)

6. Once you are logged in – enter a title for your ad

7. Enter a specific location – either your hometown or if you're doing virtual bookkeeping enter "anywhere"

8. Enter your ad under "Posting Description"

9. Hit continue and you'll be asked to verify your information

10. Your ad should appear within fifteen minutes.

Craigslist Ad Examples

On the next couple of pages are some ad examples to help you generate your own Craigslist or Kijiji ad. Make sure you don't copy them directly or your ad will be flagged and removed by Craigslist.

<u>Note:</u> If you're not comfortable using your phone number in your online ads, you can have people email you anonymously through Craigslist. Make sure you click this option when you place your ad.

Also, be careful about using your primary email as you may find your spam count increasing.

I suggest you always place a link to your bookkeeping website so clients can go there to find out more about your business.

Let me help you with your small business bookkeeping.

11 years of full cycle experience in Simply Accounting.

Pick up and drop off available.

*Accounts Payable

*Accounts Receivable

*Payroll

*Invoicing

*Remittances

*Bank Reconciliations

Concentrate on running your business and leave the bookkeeping to me. Please email [Name] with any questions through Craigslist or on our website at www.yourwebsite.com

Are you looking for a bookkeeper who will get your books done properly for a change? Someone who can sort out the confusion of your business? Someone who understands your business?

Offering full bookkeeping services, including government remittances, from a bookkeeper with a vast knowledge base of most business concerns.

Offsite and remote solutions with real time updating of your computer-based bookkeeping software. We come to you!

We can take care of all your bookkeeping needs:
-Setting up Chart of Accounts & computer based software (QuickBooks, Simply Accounting, etc)
-Accounts Receivable
-Accounts Payable
-Payroll
-Government Remittances
-Bank Reconciliations
-Year-end prep
-Messy books cleanup

Call [Name] 555-555-5555 or 555-111-5555
Email: name@yourwebsite.com
Website: www.yourwebsite.com

eBay Classified Ads

I probably don't have to tell you how massively popular eBay is. But did you know that you can place classified ads on eBay for about $10 a month?

If you provide a link to your bookkeeping website or Squidoo lens, you've got inexpensive traffic and tons of potential bookkeeping client traffic.

TIP: Just doing bookkeeping for eBay sellers alone could keep you extremely busy for a long time, so don't be afraid to contact them.

Chapter 7: Freelance Websites

"As a small businessperson, you have no greater leverage than the truth."

John Greenleaf Whittier

How to Use Freelance Sites

When you post an ad in a newspaper or elsewhere, you're putting your business information in front of as many people as possible in hopes of finding a couple targeted prospects.

Freelance sites or job boards like eLance.com operate a little differently. While many of them do allow you to post a traditional advertisement, you'll also find employers posting projects, looking for someone who can complete the job. You can land these jobs by placing bids and submitting proposals.

In other words, this is an extremely targeted market because you have a business owner with cash-in-hand, actively seeking bookkeeping services. All you have to do is convince him or her that you're the best person for the job.

While different freelancing boards operate under slightly different formats – and some of these sites tend to offer more bookkeeping jobs than others – we're going to start by talking, in general, about how you can use these sites to land freelance bookkeeping jobs. Then we'll take a look at four of the top sites.

Here's how to use these sites:

Register Your Account

Your first step is to register on these freelancing sites. Most of these sites offer a free "basic" membership, which allows you to browse and bid on a limited number of projects each month.

When you upgrade, you get perks such as being able to bid on more projects.

Should you upgrade? In most cases, the answer is yes. However, you can test out these sites first to see which ones bring you the most business. Then upgrade if it makes sense financially.

Create Your Profile

Your next step is to fill out your profile. While the exact profile fields vary among sites, generally you'll find a place to put your photo, name, location, contact information, testimonials and references, your skills and strengths, what you can do for business owners, and more information about you.

You should fill in as much of this information as possible. That's because the business owners who are considering hiring you are likely to base their decision (in part) on your profile. Basically, they want to get as much information about you as they can. If a prospective client is deciding between two equally qualified people – one with a detailed profile and one without – the business owner is likely to choose the person with the detailed profile.

> **TIP**: Be sure to include your photo. Doing so helps "humanize" you and puts a face to your name. It makes you seem more familiar. And since people like to do business with those they know, like, and trust, this photo will indirectly help you win more bids.

Just because your profile is basically an "about me" page doesn't mean it should actually be about you. That's because small business owners don't really care about you. Instead, they care about their businesses and how you can help them solve their business problems.

In other words, almost everything you put in your profile should somehow directly relate to your prospects and solving their bookkeeping problems.

Let me give you a specific example:

Here's an "about me" statement: "I have twelve years of bookkeeping experience."

That's actually an okay statement, because it tells the prospect that you didn't just roll out of school yesterday. Experience is important. But you can make this "reader-centric" by telling the prospect why those twelve years of experience are important.

Like this...

Here's a better "about you" statement: "You can take advantage of my twelve years of bookkeeping experience – if I can't solve your bookkeeping problems, no one can."

Start Browsing and Bidding

Once your profile is complete, you're ready to start looking for suitable bookkeeping jobs and bidding on them.

There are usually two ways to find these jobs on the sites:

1. Browse the correct category. Most freelance sites have their projects filed into numerous categories, so you can easily find all the bookkeeping jobs. Note that you may find them in different categories, such as "accountant" and even "data entry."

2. Search using terms like "bookkeeper" and "accountant." Keep in mind that sometimes prospects don't always use the right terminology (thus the jobs don't come up in your search), which is why you should browse categories as well as search for jobs using multiple search terms.

Usually when you bid you also send a proposal along with your bid. You'll find out more about writing a winning proposal in the next section. But first, let's talk about how much you should bid…

First off, there are always going to be business owners who shop around based on price alone. Unless you've positioned yourself as a low-priced alternative to other bookkeepers, these business owners aren't really your prospects. Instead, you're looking for people who can appreciate the special skill set, background, and experience you bring to the table… and they're willing to pay for it.

However, when you're just starting out on a freelancing site, you may have to lower your usual rates just to win more jobs. That's because prospective clients often look at a freelancer's history and feedback rating on the site. If you don't have any established history on the site and you don't have any feedback whatsoever, many prospects aren't going to take a chance on you (especially if your bid is higher than many other bids).

As such, you may consider submitting proposals with low bids just to get more work. If you do a good job with these clients, they'll leave you positive feedback. In turn, this positive feedback helps you land more clients. And before you know it, you can land jobs at your usual rates.

Now let's talk about how to create your proposal.

Submitting a Winning Proposal

When you bid on a project, you get a chance to submit a proposal. This is where you tell the prospective client why you're the right person for the job. In other words, you sell yourself.

This is where a lot of freelancers make a mistake, and I urge you not to make this same mistake. Specifically, don't create a "cookie cutter" proposal that you copy and paste into every proposal you send. Instead, make it personal. Take time to learn more about the company and the specific job, and then write a proposal that's clearly not a "copy and paste" job.

Here's how:

Get Your Proposal in Early

When you see a posted project that you like, submit your proposal ASAP. That's because most sites list proposals in the order they're given, so early submissions will be at the top of the list.

Write a Sales Letter

That's right, your proposal is basically a short sales letter. And that means most sales letter rules apply, such as:

- **List benefits.** Your proposal should answer the one burning question that's on your prospect's mind: Why should he or she hire you instead of the other bookkeepers who are bidding on the job?

  One way to do that is by offering a list of the benefits of hiring you (preferably in an easy-to-read bulleted list). Refer to the section in this book on writing sales letters for tips about how to write benefit statements.

  Another way to do that is to mention your USP (Unique Selling Proposition). This is a statement that tells prospects why you are different and better than your competitors. For example, do you offer fast turnaround? Phone consultations? "Do it right or it's free" guarantees?

  Whatever it is that sets you apart from your competition, be sure to mention it in your proposal.

- *Offer proof.* You can say you're a good bookkeeper with a lot of qualifications and experience, but the prospect would rather hear it from someone else. That means you should provide testimonials, references, and other proof whenever applicable. This is especially important if you haven't yet built up a feedback rating on the freelancing site.

- *Be enthusiastic.* The prospect wants to feel like you're not only qualified to handle the job, but also enthusiastic about it.

- *Provide a call to action.* Don't just list the reasons why the prospect should hire you and then leave them hanging. Instead, specifically ask them to choose you for this project.

Get Personal

As mentioned, you should research the company and look closely at their job description. That way your proposal can include specific details of how you'll complete the job and help the company. The more directly your proposal speaks to a business owner's specific problem, the more likely it is the business owner will seriously consider your proposal.

Follow Up

Finally, be sure to follow up. You might use the freelance site's personal message system to reiterate your enthusiasm and why you're the best person for the job. For best results, send this follow-up message near the time the bids are closing.

TIP: You can also work on building a relationship with the prospect by asking questions via private message while the bids are still open. Naturally, you shouldn't ask silly questions solely as an excuse to send a PM, because silly questions will make you look like someone who isn't a self-starter.

Instead, scrutinize the project description carefully (to make sure your question isn't already answered in the text), and ask something thoughtful. Your question should demonstrate to the prospective client that you've thought carefully about this project and that you care about the business owner's success.

Offer Good Customer Service

Once you win a project, your goal is to complete the job as quickly and professionally as possible. If you offer good work and good customer service, not only will you get good feedback ratings, you're also likely to get repeat business.

Keep these tips in mind:

- Thank the client for choosing you. You can also use this as an opportunity to reiterate your enthusiasm for the job (as well as reassure the client that he or she picked the right person).

- Get clear on the job. Read the description again so that you know exactly what the client expects. Then touch base personally (preferably by phone) to make sure you're both on the same page.

- Communicate regularly. Some clients prefer different levels of communication, so find out what this new client expects… and then be sure to update him or her regularly.

Urge the Client to Leave Feedback

Once the job is complete, urge your client to leave feedback using the freelancing site's ratings and feedback system. You may also ask this person to provide a testimonial for your website.

Second, if this was a "one off" task, don't be afraid to ask for additional work. You can also tell the client to give your name and contact information to his or her colleagues who need a reliable bookkeeper.

Now that you have a general idea of how freelancing sites work, let's look at some of the more popular sites.

eLance.com

This site is one of the best-known and established freelancing sites on the web. It's also one of the biggest. Indeed, a quick search reveals twenty-four job posts for the search term "bookkeeper." But that's just the tip of this freelancing iceberg, because there are dozens of related job posts that don't use that specific search term.

Like many freelancing sites, eLance offers you guaranteed payment. That's because they've set up an escrow service. The person who hires you pays into this neutral account. When the job is complete, eLance releases the money to you.

While there are lots of jobs and opportunities on eLance, the downside is that this site has some of the highest fees among freelancing sites. The fees start with the membership fee, which ranges from zero to about $10 per month.

While you can sign up for their basic, no cost membership, doing so won't give you an opportunity to bid on very many projects. As such, if you intend to bid a lot, you'll need to upgrade your membership. If you upgrade one level and still don't have enough bid "allotments," you'll have to pay a separate fee every time you bid on a project.

The site also takes a commission out of your "paycheck" when you get paid by a client. Currently, their rates range from 6.75 percent to 8.75 percent of the total payment. So if you land a $200 job, eLance will keep between $13.50 and $17.50 on the transaction.

Guru.com

Guru works much the same way as eLance.com, in that you can bid on bookkeeping jobs and projects posted by business owners. This site also has a relatively large number of freelance bookkeeping jobs available – as of this writing, the search term "bookkeeper" returned fifteen results, with dozens of other related jobs available.

This site also offers safe transactions and guaranteed payment via their onsite escrow service. In other words, you never have to worry about not getting paid, provided you use their "SafePay" system (which incurs a 2 percent fee).

When you fill out your profile on this site, be sure to specify your location accurately. That's because this site offers those who are looking for freelancers the ability to search for local freelancers by entering a location. Indeed, this site puts an emphasis on employers being able to search for and request bids from freelancers, so be sure your entire profile is compelling.

iFreelance.com

This is another one of the more popular freelancing sites, but it tends to have fewer bookkeeping jobs available.

What makes this site different is the pricing. The membership fees range from $4.69 to $9 per month, with more expensive memberships giving you access to more jobs. However, that's it as far as fees, since iFreelance doesn't take a commission on your payments.

Since they don't take a commission, they also offer less protection than other sites. Specifically, you accept payment on your terms since the site doesn't offer an escrow service.

ODesk.com

At the time of writing, a search for "bookkeeper" returns fifteen results (with dozens of other related jobs when you use different search terms), which put this site on the same level as the other big sites such as Guru.com.

While most freelancing sites allow those who post projects to accept bids on a "per project" basis, ODesk does things a little differently. In fact, you'll find many jobs on this site offered on a "per hour" basis since ODesk offers service providers and employers the tools to track per-hour assignments.

This site doesn't charge you anything to join. Instead, they take a flat 10 percent fee on all your payments. Payments are guaranteed when you use their onsite escrow service.

Chapter 8: Press Releases

"You are surrounded by simple, obvious solutions that can dramatically increase your income, power, influence, and success. The problem is, you just don't see them."

Jay Abraham

Getting Press Coverage

A press release is a newsworthy story about your bookkeeping business that you submit to various media outlets ~ newspapers, radio, television, magazines, etc. If the media are interested in your story, they may just interview you on their broadcast or run your press release in their publication.

A press release follows a specific format and is sent to solicit interest in your business. It's very important to remember that a press release is not an advertisement about your business. It is a newsworthy story that the media might be interested in picking up.

When thinking of press release ideas, put yourself into the shoes of someone reading a newspaper or watching a TV show. What would they want to hear about? You need to convey that information to the reporter, editor, or producer effectively.

The most important thing to remember is…don't wait for news to happen…make it happen. Use your creativity when writing your press releases and create news.

Why Use Press Releases

There are so many reasons why press releases can be good for your bookkeeping business. Here are just a few to get your mind racing with new ideas:

The great thing about a press release campaign is that it is AFFORDABLE to the small business entrepreneur. Getting attention in the press puts small and big businesses on an even playing field.

You Can't Buy Exposure Like This

People are naturally suspicious of ads, but will take a story presented by the media as an endorsement of your business. You can end up on the front page of a newspaper or be featured on a talk show for ten minutes. Could you imagine how much it would cost to pay for an ad in spots like that? Most major newspapers don't even let you buy ad spots on the front page. And if you want a 30 second commercial on TV, you'll pay hundreds, if not thousands, of dollars.

Become a Household Name

If people hear about you in the paper frequently or they hear you on their favorite radio program, you can become a household name for your bookkeeping service. Even if they don't use your service, you are in the back of their mind when someone else is looking for a bookkeeping business just like yours.

Steady Stream of Website Traffic

When you submit a press release to various online newswires, they can spread like wildfire. They are picked up by other websites – and very frequently Google News and About.com. I'll show you where to place your release for potential inclusion on these sites.

When to Send Out a Press Release

You need a good hook for your press release to get attention. Remember to show benefits to the media's audience – Why would they be interested in this? Shift the focus away from you and self-promotion. Your audience is most important. Here are some ideas to get your creative juices flowing:

The launch of your business or website – What is unique about your bookkeeping business? What problem does it solve for people? What are the benefits to your visitors or customers?

Adding new services and products – Again, make it newsworthy. Make sure to focus on the benefits and why your target audience would be interested in the new bookkeeping service. It's all about benefits. Will it save them ten hours every week? Will it increase their income by 2 percent?

Be the expert – This can't be stressed enough. Even if you don't think you are an expert, take some time to think about it and you'll see that you are. If you can find that expert angle and build a relationship with the media, you'll have the media calling on you for your expert opinion on related stories.

Events – Announce your special events, like public speaking engagements, open houses, seminars, fairs you're arranging, etc. Create quality events just to get publicity. Be unique, set yourself apart from other events, and make sure you're contributing to the community.

Sweepstakes & contests – Write a press release about your contest or sweepstakes while it's running.

Follow-up to your sweepstakes & contests - Then send a release announcing the winners once the contest is over. Check legalities in your area.

Fundraisers and donations – If you are running a fundraiser or making a considerable donation (for example, 5 percent of your sales for the month of September), write a press release about it. It will bring attention to your business and help you run an even more successful fundraiser. Make sure your story encourages others to help you make those contributions – offer your clients an incentive, have a theme, give a little gift.

For example, if you're supporting breast cancer charities, give out a little pink candle with a pink ribbon for every purchase over a certain amount.

Follow-up on your fundraiser – When your fundraiser is progressing or is over and the results are in, send out a follow-up.

Free stuff – Do you have a great freebie on your website? Everybody loves free stuff. Whip up a press release announcing your freebie.

Community service – Do you offer training or apprenticeships to students or unemployed individuals? Does your business sponsor a local sports team? A press release is a great way to let people know about your community service.

Major awards and accomplishments – If you've been given a prestigious award, write a press release about it. Just keep in mind that a press release is not your opportunity to brag about yourself. You still need to focus on how that award shows you can help others.

Interviews you've been a part of or books you've been featured in - If an interview has been published on a website, newspaper or other media, this is a newsworthy event in itself.

Conduct surveys or statistical analyses – Survey a sector of the population on a topic of interest and report your findings in a press release.

Create a special day – Create a "National Day" for something related to your bookkeeping business.

Offer a free booklet or report – Information is very valuable. If you can create a free report on a relevant topic, people will come running. Don't forget to include some good promotion of your business in that very informative book.

With your website, you can do this in digital format – like a .pdf file, an audio mp3 or even a video – but make sure your target market is tech-savvy. Or better yet, offer a digital format and a hard copy format so that people can make their choice.

Digital is perfect for people who want their information NOW and know how to download off the Internet. Mailed information is for non-technical people or ones who prefer to have the information right in their own hands.

Open up your phone lines for support on your hot topic – This will likely take more financial resources and/or time than the booklet, but allows you a more personal approach to delivering the information.

Schedule a teleconference - You can do that for free (for up to 100 people) at **www.freeconference.com**

Tell them about your ezine – If you're starting an informative newsletter, tell the media about it.

Find a problem and solve it – If your bookkeeping service solves a problem, write a story about the problem and offer your expert advice on its solution (part of which will be your service!)

Give out awards – Sure, it's great to tell people when you get an award, but why not turn things around and offer awards to people in your community? These could be certificates, bursaries, or even scholarships.

Proper Press Release Format

Your press release should follow a specific format and include a few key components. Reporters and editors receive many releases each and every day. You only have a few seconds to grab their attention, so write a succinct and interesting story. The headline and first paragraph are often your only chance to get attention before your press release ends up in the shredder.

And Never Forget! This story is for your readers (the editor/reporter and ultimately, their audience) ~ tell them why it would interest them. You are not important.

Here's what your press release should include:

Date Instructions

"For Immediate Release";

"For Release Before [date]" or

"For Release After [date]"

Use one of the latter two if your press release is of a time sensitive nature. For example, if you're holding a public speaking event, you will want to use the "For Release Before [date]" and make sure you input the final date for registrations. If you're using the "For Release Before [date]" make sure you're sensitive to media deadlines. Send your release out well in advance.

Headline

Use an attention-grabbing headline. There's a fine line between a promotional headline and a headline that gets attention, but don't be too mundane and factual in your headline. That's boring.

Contact Information

Include as much information as possible here. Make it easy for the media to contact you. Include your phone number, address, company name, fax number, email, and URL. Include the hours you're available at the listed phone number and add an after hours phone number, if applicable.

Summary

Before you get into the body of the release, write a sentence or two to summarize your press release. Make it interesting because you want the recipient to keep reading. Also, include the area to which this release is relevant.

Content

This is the meat of your press release. Again, write a benefits-oriented story. Think of the target audience as you're writing. Your target audience is partly the editor or reporter who will be reading the release. Ultimately, however, your target audience is that editor or reporter's readers or audience. You need to write a story that will be of interest to them.

The first paragraph should answer all the important questions— Who, What, Where, When, Why and How. You only have a few seconds to keep an editor's or reporter's interest. Here's your chance.

Signify the End of Your Press Release

The end of your press release is shown by a few simple characters. Place ### at the end of your release.

Other Important Formatting Tips

- Keep your release to about one page (or two pages maximum).

- Number your pages 1 of 2, 2 of 2, etc.

- Avoid hype. Don't use big words and adjectives. Stick to the facts in plain English, ma'am.

- Focus on benefits: What problems do you solve for your customers or website visitors?

- Use bold headlines to get attention.

- Break up your paragraphs for easy reading.

- Tweak your release when sending to different media outlets. If you're sending it to the local paper, your content may be slightly different than if you're sending it to a trade journal.

- If you're sending your release by mail, use 8 1/2" x 11" letterhead. Use only one side of the paper. If your release is more than one page long, write "more" at the bottom.

- If you're sending your release by email, never send an attachment. Copy and paste your release into the body of the email.

- Back up your claims with facts and statistics. Often the media will publish your press release without interviewing you or making substantial changes. They may not even have time to check your facts, so if they're dubious, then they may just toss out your release.

Consider sending out a Press Release Kit, instead of just a simple press release.

Here's what you can include:

- Cover Letter

- Press Release(s)

- Business Fact Sheet

- Your Biography

- Samples, Photos, etc.

- Company Literature

- Your Business Card

You need to evaluate the cost of sending a full press release kit. You may want to indicate that you will send samples upon request as an alternative.

However you decide to send your release, you need to stand out from the crowd. You need to create a press release that would interest the editor and her target audience.

Create & Build a Media List

You need to build a media list and it will likely take some time to get a really good list going. If you've just begun building your media list, start locally and small. And start online so you can build traffic to your website.

Local and/or small media are most likely to be interested in your story and it's the perfect way to hone your press release writing skills. Besides, a lot of the larger media outlets scan the smaller outlets to find stories to pick up. Also, as you gain experience and build-up your portfolio, you can work your way up to bigger media outlets.

Try newspapers, trade journals, topic specific magazines, websites, radio shows, television show ~ whoever would be interested in your topic.

Always remember to get specific contact information for your press release when possible. A release addressed to a particular person will receive a lot more attention than a general release sent to the media outlet. You'll also want to update your list frequently as staff may often change.

Familiarize yourself with the editor or reporter's work. Find out the method she prefers to receive press releases in. Don't automatically send them by email — some will prefer mail or fax. Find out their deadlines.

How to Build Your Distribution List

1. For your local media, check the publication or their website for information on how to submit a release. Find out the precise editor or reporter you should be addressing your release to. You may have to pick up your phone to get this information or hire an assistant to do the calling and information gathering for you.

2. Do a search on your favorite search engine for websites in your industry that might be interested in running your story.

3. Here are a few websites to help you build your list:

www.MediaPost.com - extensive directory for U.S. media
www.NewsLink.org - directory for a number of countries
www.ABYZNewsLinks.com - directory for a number of countries

> **TIP:** If you choose a free resource to build your list, realize that the information may not always be completely up-to-date. A paid resource will often provide more current information and if they don't, ask them for a refund!

4. Submit your site to a few online newswires and news websites. A number of them require payment, but here are some, both free and paid.

www.PRWeb.com - They do a great job, but no longer offer a free service.

www.PressMethod.com - Free press release distribution center.

www.PRFree.com - Free press release distribution

www.24-7PressRelease.com - Free service. You can also contribute funds to receive better placement for your release.

Extra Exposure from Google and About.com

Google.com often takes press releases from PRWeb.com. You may be buried in their news section, BUT if someone searches for keywords on Google related to your press release topic...your release may be featured at the top of the results.

About.com also scours press releases to add to its various sections and you might just find yourself listed without submitting to them. If you're not familiar with About.com, they are a huge website with information on just about every topic there could possibly be. I've had press releases and articles listed there and they can bring you tons of extra traffic on an ongoing basis. If you think your press release should be listed, contact the editor of the appropriate section and suggest your press release for inclusion...or you can just ask them to list your website as a resource.

More Potential Resources

Magazines, Newspapers & Radio Programs: You can also search places like **magazines.com** and **newspapers.com** for ideas on target publications. The focus of these websites is not to build a media list, so you'll have to do some digging for the appropriate contact information. Still, you might find publications you won't find in the other resources.

www.magazines.com
www.newspapers.com
www.radio-locator.com (radio stations with websites)
www.npr.org/stations (National Public Radio member stations in the U.S.)

Internet Radio: Although the distribution is probably not as great as with mainstream radio, you may want to search targeted programs on Internet radio. Here are a few places to look:

www.live365.com
www.penguinradio.com
www.worldtalkradio.com
www.wsradio.com

Websites: Do a Google search for websites listed for your target keywords. Find websites that tend to be informational and deliver content to their visitors. You can also search directories such as:

dir.yahoo.com
www.dmoz.org

Creative Ways to Get Publicity

A press release is the traditional way to gain publicity for your business, but it may not always be the best way. Here are a few creative ways to gain free publicity for your business.

Pick up the Phone

Reporters are busy, but sometimes a personal touch will work. You may also make that call at just the right time. The reporter may have a deadline looming and space to fill.

Use your judgment when making phone calls. Don't try to get Diane Sawyer on the phone, but if you'd like a spot on a local radio show, why not give the host or producer a call? Besides, radio is a very verbal media and they want to hear your voice and see if you'd be a suitable guest. If you do call, show you're serious and don't use the 1-800 number.

Send a Personal Email to a Website Publisher

If you're looking to be interviewed by a website publisher, check her submission guidelines. She may appreciate a personal email instead of a formal press release. It shows you took the time to write that publisher instead of sending "canned" information about your business. Take the time to talk about the publisher's own website and speak in very specific terms.

Don't send the same message to a number of publishers. Experienced publishers will know when they're being sent a form letter.

Letters to the Editor

You can send letters to the editor to promote your bookkeeping business. If you read a story on a subject in your expertise, send in your opinion. Word it so people know who you are and what you're doing.

Example: "As a bookkeeper for ten years, I find your story on....", and if you can, sneak in your business name in the signature.

Again...be the expert!

Speak at Public Events

Volunteer for speaking engagements at public events. This will help establish you as an expert in your field.

What to Do When a Reporter Calls

So, you sent in your press release and guess what? A reporter calls and she wants to run your story. Be enthusiastic, but stay calm...you'll get through this. Hopefully, you're already prepared for this call with the following:

- A list of points you would like to cover in an interview.

- Documentation with supporting information—for your reference and to send to the reporter if she requests it.

Here are a few tips on what to do and ask when a reporter calls:

Grab a pen and paper and write down the important details, including:

- Reporter's name and phone number

- Which publication or broadcast; time, date, and location of interview, if it isn't going to take place right then on the telephone

1. Find out what angle the reporter wants to take on the story. Make certain that this angle will be favorable to your business or illustrates your expertise.

2. If you feel you need preparation, ask for a few sample questions that will be covered.

3. Ask if your website URL will be published in the interview. After all, the purpose of sending your press release was for publicity. If they won't publish your URL, you'll have to decide whether the interview will be worth the exposure for you or not. If this is one of your first interviews, you might want to jump at the chance for experience.

What If It's Not A Good Time?

If the reporter calls at an inconvenient time, or if you're not quite ready, ask if you can call back shortly. Gather your thoughts and documentation and call back promptly. If your kids are screaming and you're sure to be flustered, it's a much better idea to call the reporter back.

If the Interview Will Take Place in the Future

Announce your coverage on your website and make an announcement to your newsletter subscribers. Tell them where they will be able to listen to or read your interview. It definitely adds credibility to your image and helps create trust with your readers.

How to Handle the Interview

Congratulations! Don't forget to breathe...everything will be fine. Just remember a few key points and you'll do great.

Take a moment to think about your answers – especially if the interview will be edited or put into print. And remember, what seems like an eternity-long silence to you is likely only a couple of seconds.

1. Speak in plain English. Don't use technical jargon and explain any industry-specific terms you do use.

2. Speak in a friendly, yet convincing manner. Hide those nerves and be sure of yourself. After all, you're being interviewed because you are the expert.

3. Back up your claims with facts and give examples.

4. If you don't understand a question, ask for clarification.

5. If you don't know the answer to a question, you can say, "I don't know offhand, but I can certainly find out that information."

6. Don't speak "off the record." You can never be certain that it won't end up in the interview.

Tips for Television Interviews

- Wear solid colored clothing. Patterns can be quite distracting on television.
- Look at the reporter, not the camera.

If You Have to Send More Information after the Interview

- Find out the preferred method: fax, mail, email, etc.
- Ask the reporter's deadline and ensure the information gets there in time.

After the Interview

Announce your coverage on your website and make an announcement to your newsletter subscribers. If possible, link to the story or offer a transcript.

Always keep the contact information of the reporter or whoever ran your story. Be sure to thank him after your story runs and contact him personally when you have a new story.

Press Release Examples

You'll find real-live press release examples put together by **PRWeb.com** here:

http://service.prweb.com/who-uses-it

Read through these examples to really get a good idea of the format of a press release, the way they are written, and how they promote a business or a person – without sounding like an ad.

PRWeb.com also provides tips and daily one hour webinars on writing press releases that are worth checking out. You can find them here:

http://service.prweb.com/

TIP: For a free "Press Release Template" to help you create your own press release go to:

www.GetBookeepingClients.com/gbc-resources.html

Chapter 9: Offline Networking

"It's all about people. It's about networking and being nice to people and not burning any bridges."

Mike Davidson

Offline Networking Tips

Getting Referrals From Other Bookkeepers

Many established solo bookkeepers find they reach a point where they can't take on any more work because they're booked solid.

If you've managed to contact these bookkeepers ahead of time and let them know you're available for any overflow work, you'll be in a great position to benefit from their referrals.

The way to do this is to call other bookkeepers and introduce yourself. Tell them that you're just starting out and are looking for clients. Many times you can get very good leads this way. Leave your name and phone number with them, or send them your business card along with a friendly letter reminding them of your conversation.

Also, make sure you talk to everyone you come in contact with and tell them about your bookkeeping business. Just ask them to recommend you if they know anyone who is looking for a bookkeeper.

Join Business Groups

Consider joining your local Chamber of Commerce, Rotary Club, or other such business networking group. These groups usually have regular networking meetings or events so people in business can make contact with one another. Make sure you attend as many functions as you can.

Have an "elevator speech" ready for when you meet a prospective client. An elevator speech is your 30 second soundbite introducing who you are and what you do.

Contact Payroll Companies

If you're familiar with payroll companies, this can work to your advantage. Not only can you help your bookkeeping clients by providing professional payroll services for these companies, but you can also benefit from this as well.

Just contact these payroll companies and offer to send clients their way if they'll in turn send any potential bookkeeping clients to you. It's win-win for both of you.

Become a Consultant

Many bookkeepers become so proficient at using their accounting software that they decide to become consultants for the software itself. This is a great way to find bookkeeping clients as well as make some additional money helping others learn the software.

Both QuickBooks and Simply Accounting provide this option. They will even list you as a consultant on their sites to help drive clients to you.

Referrals From Existing Clients

Word of mouth is always the best form of advertising. Not only is it free, but getting an unbiased referral about your business from a satisfied client is more persuasive than any advertising you could ever create on your own.

Some clients will refer businesses to you on their own, but many times it will be up to you to request referrals. You can do this a couple of ways:

- Mention that you're looking for more clients in casual conversations with your client and ask them to let others know that you're available.

- Offer a discount to current clients if they send someone your way who ends up becoming a client. Alternatively you can offer gift certificates or coupons as an incentive.

- Add a notation to your monthly invoice mentioning the referral special.

Chapter 10: Online Networking

"Looking at the proliferation of personal web pages on the Net, it looks like very soon everyone on Earth will have 15 megabytes of fame."

M.G. Sriram

Online Networking

Social sites like **Twitter.com, Facebook.com,** and **Squidoo.com** have become hot and are getting hotter all the time. Both online and offline businesses are jumping into social marketing – and for a good reason. It works.

To push past your competition, you'll want to continually build relationships and stay ever-present in the marketplace. Social media can help you to accomplish this. And, it's fun.

Thankfully, there are simple and effective ways to use these social Web 2.0 sites. I'll share some of those tips with you now.

Twitter

Many people are using Twitter as a way to connect with colleagues, family, friends, and customers. If you haven't tried Twitter, now may be the time to set up an account and see what it's all about. Twitter is a "micro blogging" platform where you can write in 140 characters or less anything you'd like. You can update people about your day, share resources, send a link to your website — anything that you feel your followers will find useful or interesting.

When you're a member of Twitter, you "follow" people and they "follow" you.

This means that when you log in to your Twitter account, you will see the messages posted by those who you're following. Likewise, the people who have decided to follow you will see your messages.

> **Example:** Sally follows Paul. So, when Sally logs into her Twitter account, she can see Paul's updates on her screen along with all of the other people she's following.

To use Twitter for marketing your bookkeeping business, the people you follow and those who follow you should be highly targeted. They log in because they're interested in what you and others have to say. Since there are only 140 characters allowed per "Tweet" (Twitter post), you'll want to encourage your followers to follow your link for more information on what you're referring to.

If you use this social media site in the correct way, you'll gain loyal followers, which leads to targeted traffic and then some very targeted clients. Some have even found Twitter traffic to be more targeted than Pay Per Click and article marketing, both of which are proven methods of Internet marketing.

TIP: To learn more about using this popular social networking platform, look for the ebook called **"Twitter Traffic"** here:

www.GetBookkeepingClients.com/gbc-resources.html

Facebook

Facebook is a social media site that started out as a way for college friends to keep in contact. Soon high school students signed on and later everyone age thirteen and older became eligible to become a member. Now Facebook is being used for business as well. It seems that everyone you run into today has a Facebook page. As of this writing, Facebook has over 500 million active users. That's a whole lot of potential traffic.

Just like you have followers on Twitter, you have friends on Facebook and that's where the power of Facebook lies.

You can update your status, link to your website, and leave comments on your friends' Facebook pages. Again, this creates a great community feeling as well as very targeted traffic since people will get to know you and become interested in your opinions and suggestions before clicking through a link to your website.

> **TIP:** Look for the free ebook called "Facebook for Business" here:
>
> **www.GetBookkeepingClients.com/gbc-resources.html**

Digg

Digg is a very interesting way to receive traffic, and it is currently favored by Google. The basic idea is that when you enjoy or really "dig" an article, you "Digg" it. If other people are interested, they will Digg it as well by clicking the "Digg" button that appears. The more Diggs a web page receives, the higher the rankings and exposure tends to be.

You can Digg your own articles and web pages on your site as long as you are careful. Digg has banned users for spamming or being too self-promotional. However, if you use the true social aspect of it by making friends, digging their articles, and digging great articles you find online you can easily drive targeted traffic to your own submissions as well.

Linked In

Linked In may be classified as an "unusual" social media site as compared to Twitter, Facebook, or Digg. While those sites tend to promote finding old friends and making new ones while networking socially, Linked In is geared to the world of business networking.

Using it will help you network within your chosen niche for suggestions, support, and help. It will also allow you to search other niches and find targeted prospects as well.

Linked In is similar to Facebook in one way—you'll be given a Linked In "page" where you can post information about your business and the reason you are there. You can add business websites, blog addresses, and anything else related to your business.

As of this writing more than 75 million professionals worldwide regularly use Linked In. Just think of how many people you could reach out to about your business. Linked In is definitely a great social site for all business owners to become members of.

Social sites put an exciting spin on website promotion and marketing. Not only are you getting fantastic exposure to your online business, you're also having fun as a part of a greater community of friends and business associates.

Other Social Media

Here's a list of some other social media sites that you can use to promote your bookkeeping business:

- www.meetup.com
- giantpotential.ning.com
- www.ryze.com
- www.everywoman.com
- www.business-scene.com
- econnect.entrepreneur.com
- www.ukbusinessforums.co.uk/forums
- www.viadeo.com/en/connexion
- www.friendster.com
- www.xing.com
- www.wibn.co.uk

Online Business Directories

Online business directories are usually very cheap,or even free. You can easily set up a listing for your bookkeeping business that links to either your email or your website or Squidoo lens.

You can find these directories by Googling:

"city" + business

You can also post your ads on online bookkeeping directories. Just Google "bookkeeping directory" to find them.

> **TIP**:   You can list your bookkeeping business for only $25/month at www.BookkeeperWanted.net, which is a directory of bookkeepers from all over North America and Australia.

Using Forums

Although online business owners are being dazzled by social media sites like Facebook and Twitter, the old-style method of participating in highly-targeted forums or message boards is still one of the most effective traffic-generation methods used today. Your link can be prominently displayed in front of the exact audience you're attempting to lure. Don't overlook this strategy. You may be surprised with the results it still brings in.

The following four tips will ensure that you are using forums effectively and to the best advantage of your bookkeeping business.

Choose Wisely

Forums are extremely popular on the Internet. You're likely to find a forum on any subject you can think of, from fantasy baseball to purses. Because of the abundance of forums, you should be very picky when choosing which ones you'll frequent and post on. This will save you time and allow you to achieve optimum results.

You should decide on a forum that relates either directly or indirectly to your chosen bookkeeping market, but there must be a connection. Otherwise, your posts will be a time-waster. In fact, the more you can "niche down" your topic, the most effective your marketing will be.

For instance, if you're targeting Internet marketers, then you'll want to go to forums where these types of people hang out. To find a forum in your chosen market, just Google "keyword + forum," with the keyword being your chosen market.

Read the Rules

Your next step after deciding on a forum to join is to read the rules of the forum. There are forums that may not allow you to include a signature file (where you would put a link to your website) at all. Others have rules that dictate how many posts you need to have before you can add a signature file. Some allow zero marketing – so you should skip those.

Once you read the rules, remember to adhere to them no matter what. If you violate these rules in any way, you may be pegged as a nuisance and kicked out of the forum, while possibly ruining your reputation and wasting your time.

As long as you're a valued contributing member of the forum offering great advice and content, more often than not you will be able to include a link to your site in your posts.

Create a Compelling Signature File

After choosing a forum or two and familiarizing yourself with their rules, it's time to decide what you want your forum signature file to express about you. Since you want people to click through to your bookkeeping website, you need to make sure that your signature line is targeted and entices people to learn more about you.

This is a wise opportunity to utilize your copywriting skills. Make sure those one or two sentences gets prospects' attention and curiosity as well as alerts prospects that you may be able to solve a pending problem of theirs.

Giving away something for free will help entice people to click on your signature link. So this would be a good place to give away your free ecourse or a free report.

It's wise to test your signature file and tweak it to see which advertisement gets the best results. Keeping it fresh also gives the added benefit of attracting the eyes of those who've gotten used to your old ads.

Build Trust

People may be a bit suspicious of new members when they first join a forum. There is a dynamic in any forum, and believe it or not, cliques often form. If you hope to get people to click on your signature file and eventually buy from you, you'll need to earn their trust first.

There are many different ways to accomplish this, and you can get an idea for which way is best by looking at the profiles and posts of the most prolific and respected members.

Examples of how you may build trust with forum members include:

- Having a profile picture.
- Using a real name (or a real sounding pen name) as your username.
- Filling out general information in your profile such as where you live and your birth date.
- Including some personal information in your profile bio to make you seem like a real person they can relate to.

People generally want to know something about who they are speaking to or considering doing business with.

Forums can be a source of highly-targeted web traffic when used smartly and correctly. Choosing a related forum, following the rules, creating a strong signature file, and proving that you can be trusted are all excellent ways to ensure that you'll get traffic to your website and benefit from increased "expert" status while networking in online communities.

TIP: For a free report called **"Forum Marketing Techniques"** go here:

www.GetBookkeepingClients.com/gbc-resources.html

Using YouTube

YouTube is a great way to showcase your bookkeeping business and knowledge. This online video site gets millions of visitors and has a massive following of dedicated viewers. Often you can get your video listed on the first page of Google simply by using relevant keywords.

The key is to generate traffic from YouTube to your bookkeeping website, blog or Squidoo lens. You do this by simply add your URL to the video itself.

How to Make a YouTube Video

Although the process of making a YouTube video may seem like a complicated one, it doesn't have to be. Even those with a low amount of computer knowledge are able to successfully make their own videos, many of which later end up on YouTube.

The first step in making a YouTube video is to get a video recording device. Video recording devices come in a number of different formats. For instance, it is possible to use cell phones, webcams, or traditional camcorders.

If you're interested in using your cell phone to help you make a YouTube video, make sure yours has video recording capabilities. You will find that most new, modern cell phones do. For the best quality videos, you should use traditional camcorders, particularly digital ones, but webcams are also nice, low cost alternatives.

Popular videos on YouTube include video blogs, comedy skits, how-to videos, and travel videos. However, you can make just about any type of video you want, whether it's one that's staged or simply recording spur of the moment activities or conversations.

When making a YouTube video, it's important to remember that YouTube doesn't limit the number of videos you can submit, but all videos must be ten minutes or less if you have a traditional YouTube membership account. Therefore, if you want to have videos be longer than ten minutes, you either need to upgrade your account or make your videos in different segments.

When making your YouTube video, you'll want to make sure that the quality is good. For this, it is a good idea to speak directly into the camera or else use raised voices. This will help ensure that those watching your videos on YouTube can actually understand what you're saying.

It's also advised that you make sure the lighting is good. The best time to make movies is during the day. If you want to make your movies at night, whether they take place inside or outdoors, you'll want to make sure that you have the appropriate amount of lighting. No one wants to watch a video that is hard to see.

Although there are a number of steps, like the ones mentioned above, that you can take to ensure that your YouTube videos are quality ones, there is a way that you can fix problems later on. You can do this with movie editing software.

Movie editing software allows you to preview and edit your videos, should you wish to do so before uploading them to YouTube. If you have a relatively new computer, you should be able to find movie editing software already on your computer. If you are unable to find movie editing software, you should be able to get free software programs or even purchase deluxe software programs online or from one of your local media stores.

You'll want to watch your videos and see if there's anything you'd like to edit, change, or remove. If so, the time to do it is before you post your video on the YouTube website. Editing your YouTube videos or at least previewing them first is likely to improve their quality, which, in turn, will help improve the exposure that your YouTube videos get.

Many YouTube members share videos that they find interesting with those that they know and your videos may be one of them.

Ideas For Content

The purpose of your video is to inform and intrigue your viewer with content they find compelling enough to entice them go to your URL and learn more about your bookkeeping services. Here are some ideas for videos:

- What they should look for in hiring a bookkeeper
- Why hiring a freelance bookkeeper is more cost effective than they might think
- Any new tax changes that affect small businesses
- The difference between a bookkeeper and an accountant (almost all businesses owners are confused by this)

The most important thing to remember is that your video should not be a direct advertisement for your bookkeeping business. Instead it should inform the viewer without boring them.

Chapter 11: Article Marketing

"If you're attacking your market from multiple positions and your competition isn't, you have all the advantage and it will show up in your increased success and income."

Jay Abraham

Article Marketing

Article marketing is a great way to market your bookkeeping business. However, if you plan to use these articles online or want to submit them to Article Directories (such as www.EzineArticles.com) you'll have to make sure you use original articles.

TIP: For twenty prewritten articles that you can use to promote your bookkeeping business, go here:

www.GetBookkeepingClients.com/enhanced.html

Writing Your Own Articles

There are many ways to get your articles noticed and in the hands of potential bookkeeping clients. I'm going to give you four specific areas to focus on that will greatly improve the odds that your articles will be read, and at the same time will create a relationship with your prospects that can last a lifetime.

Know What You're Talking About

Research is a word that many people dread. Most of those who shy away from research have yet to recognize its true value. If they did, I'm willing to bet they would change their tune on the subject. In order to come up with quality information for your reader, you will want to do research to come up with new ideas and find the latest theories and trends in your niche.

A lot of people assume reading a few blurbs about a subject here and there is enough to write a quality article. That is far from the truth. In order to really give your readers what they want to know, you'll want to dig deeper.

Determine who the experts in your specific area are, find out what they have to say on the subject, and take a look at the items they are recommending. Do as much as you can to get background information and facts.

If possible, interview these experts to learn more. This also will provide you with original, fresh quotes that you can use in your article.

Researching your content improves credibility and expertise. You'll be able to present quality content people will want to read and continue to come back for.

Clear the Cobwebs and Stay Focused

One of the smartest steps you can take when writing an article is to create an outline before you begin. This will help you stay organized and on track. It works wonders for focus too.

An outline doesn't have to be extremely in-depth or comprehensive. Start off by planning the introduction, add a few key points for the body, and finish up with a conclusion or miniature summary of your article's main points. Here's a little trick writers use to create their outlines:

1. Tell your readers what you're going to be talking about. (Introduction)
2. Talk about it. (Body)
3. Recap what you just told them. (Conclusion)

If you're thinking that putting together an outline will only create more work for yourself, think again. In all actuality, it will save you time in the long run. Your thoughts will be organized and you'll be able to focus on each individual piece of the puzzle that, when complete, will flow together nicely.

Spice Things Up with a Dash of Copy

The most important function of any article is to inform its reader. But, your article must get and keep their attention in order to inform, right?

Many people neglect to focus on the fact articles need to be compelling, but they also need to sell your services. There are many elements of copy you can include to make your articles compelling and lead people to a certain action. You can create interest and increase action with things like:

• Attention grabbing headlines and subheadings. (These draw the reader in and leave them wanting to know more.)

• A hook line. (This will keep them reading.)

Keep in mind that everyone is very busy these days; if you want to get your article read from beginning to end, you will have a higher chance of success when you add a bit of creative copywriting.

Article Topics to Write About

Since the goal in writing articles is to generate traffic to your bookkeeping website, blog or Squidoo lens, what you write about is important. Here are some topics to get you started:

- Why a freelance bookkeeper is more cost-effective than hiring an employee.

- Why "shoebox bookkeeping" is a bad idea for small business owners.

- What qualities to look for in a freelance bookkeeper.

- How virtual bookkeeping is more convenient for the home business owner.

Lead Your Readers Onward

If you remember nothing else about people who read your articles, remember this:

You must TELL your reader what to do next!

Yes, we humans are fickle creatures. Even if your reader thinks she knows what to do next, that doesn't mean she will do it. Always remember to tell your readers what to do or where to go after they've finished reading your article. Because, believe it or not, even when they know what they want or what they should be doing next, people are indecisive. Like a child who is just learning the ways of the world, your reader needs to be taken by the hand and led to the next step.

For instance, if you want your reader to visit your website to learn more about your bookkeeping business, send them there. If you'd like your reader to complete a survey or give his opinion on the topic he's just finished reading about, tell him where to go to do so.

You don't do any self-promotion in the article itself. You do this only in the author or resource box at the bottom of the article. Use this area to tell a bit about yourself or your website, and give your readers something to do. Give them a clear call to action.

Writing an article is not difficult as long as you put the right strategies in place. Know what information is relevant to your target audience. Be as well versed in the area you're writing about as you can in order to provide superior information.

Distributing Your Article

Once you've written your article, you'll need to publish it online in order to generate traffic to your bookkeeping website or blog. The easiest way to do this is to submit your article to an online article directory.

Here are some online directories:

- EzineArticles.om
- ArticlesBase.com
- GoArticles.com
- ArticleAlley.com

There are hundreds of these directories online that you can find by Googling "article directories".

Alternatively, you can also simply publish your articles to your own blog or add them to your Squidoo lens. However, you should be aware that if you choose to do both, some article directories (such as EzineArticles.com) will not accept your article if it's published elsewhere. To get around this, simply publish your article at EzineArticles first and then publish it whereover you like.

TIP: EzineArticles now has a "plugin" that you can upload to your blog so that everytime you post to your blog your article is automatically submitted to their article directory.

Chapter 12: Blogs

"Obviously everyone wants to be successful, but I want to be looked back on as being very innovative, very trusted and ethical, and ultimately making a big difference in the world."

Sergey Brin

Blogs for Business

Blogging has become extremely popular over the last few years. Using a blog to promote your bookkeeping website is a smart method in getting traffic and ultimately, potential clients.

You can either set up a separate WordPress blog to promote your bookkeeping website or if you're using WordPress as your bookkeeping website, you can simply add a blog section.

It's important to start off on the right foot so you don't become discouraged. Here are some tips to get you headed in the right direction.

Plan Your Blogging

One mistake that people make is blogging when they feel like it — whatever is in their heads at that moment in time. This is fine if you are just journaling for your own benefit, but if you would like to gain an audience and an income, a bit of planning is key.

When you plan your blog, you should consider the categories, pages, and what you want to include in each of your posts. It would also be beneficial to make a posting schedule and stick to it, whether that's once a day, once a week, or a few times each month. Your schedule may need tweaking as time goes on, but starting with one from the beginning will lay a good foundation for your blog success.

Remember to carefully select your keywords if you're trying to rank high in the search engines. Newer bloggers will find it easiest to choose long keyword phrases related to the niche that have less competition in the search engines than single words. (Example: "how to get more followers on Twitter" would be easier to rank than "Twitter" would be.)

Finding Great Content for Your Blog

In order to make your blog successful, you'll need to get traffic to it and keep them coming back. The best way to do this is to provide the best content you can and make it interesting to your blog readers.

Even the most successful bloggers start to run out of their own original content to post about. Some resort to scraping the bottom of the barrel to find things to discuss, but that ultimately loses them readers, which means less traffic to your bookkeeping website.

Where do you find great ideas to post about? There are actually many different things to use to get you out of your stuck-in-a-rut mode. These may be simple techniques to use, but they can be effective if used right.

Here are some things to try the next time you get stuck for something to write about:

Scour the news sites - Search the news sites like CNN, MSNBC, and FOXNEWS and see if you can find a top story that you can blog about. Instead of just linking to the story, add your own accounting of it. You can post about your personal feelings toward the story or ask your readers what their thoughts are on it. Just make sure the story somehow relates to your blog's topic.

Check out your fellow blogger's sites and see what they're blogging about – It may seem unethical, but as long as you're not stealing content, it's perfectly acceptable to see what the community is interested in. Is there a post that catches your eye? Is there something you can add to that post? A new spin you can put on it? Media outlets always have an eye on the competition to see what others are doing – and you should, too!

Internet research - Do a search on the Internet for your blog's topic. See what information you can come up with concerning your niche. You may become inspired by something you've read there or you may think of some comments to post about it.

Join Google's experimental search option that lets you search in different ways – including timeline, information lists, and mapping details. This can give you more ideas than the traditional search route:

www.google.com/experimental/index.html

Check the video sites - YouTube has a zillion different videos out there that you can add to your blog. See if you can find one that relates to your blog's topic. Post the video to your blog and have your readers share their thoughts on it.

Consider doing reviews - Reviews can be a good filler to use while you try to get inspired again. Choose some articles, websites, books, or whatever you can think of that's related to your blog's topic and post a review of it. If it's a good review, add your affiliate link and make some money from your opinions!

Daily activities - Think about what happened within your day that you might be able to work into your blog. As you do your bookkeeping work, write down topics that pop into your mind that might be good for your blog readers.

You can also write about:

- New tax legislation in your area and how it will affect small businesses.
- How business owners can save money by spending some time organizing the paperwork they submit to their bookkeeper better.
- Any methods you've discovered to help lower business owners' operating expenses.

You can easily get back your inspiration for your blog posting if you look to other sources. They can help you come up with ideas of what you can share with your readers or they can give you a nice filler until your personal inspiration comes back. Don't lose readers just because you've lost your blogging muse!

Choosing a Site for Your Blog

For those just starting out in the blogging business, you're probably wondering which site is best to start your blog with. The three most popular blogging sites that most bloggers choose for their business needs are Blogger, WordPress, and LiveJournal.

Not all blogging sites are good for advertisements, so you'll want to check each one out. Here's a short comparison of the three sites listed here to help you choose what's best for you and your niche:

Blogger.com - This is usually the choice for beginners because it's the easiest of the three to set up. Simply sign up for an account and it takes you step by step through the process of getting a blog started.

Blogger is affiliated with Google, so even signing up for the AdSense ads is extremely easy to do. There aren't as many blog templates to choose from as the others, but this site is definitely recommended for those with no blogging experience who want to get launched without hassle.

WordPress.com - As previously discussed on page 29, WordPress offers plenty of different blog templates to choose from and many people create free templates you can download as long as the bottom of the blog gives them credit. This is perfect because when you're promoting to a niche audience, the theme can set the tone and authority of the site for the reader.

LiveJournal.com - This is an excellent community-driven blogging site. It offers a free account to blog with as well as a paid account option. Unfortunately, you have to upgrade to a paid account to use most of its features.

Ads are a paid account benefit, so this option isn't the best choice for making money from ads with little to no start-up cost. Advertisers can pay you to place ads on your blog if you have a paid account.

The free account is good for use as a networking tool to get others to visit your blog on another site where you could make money. Consider it a "feeder blog" that funnels readers through to another destination.

There are many other blogging sites out there to choose from, but most offer paid accounts to utilize the best services they have. Going with a free account now is the best option when you want to keep costs low and earning potential high.

You can always upgrade later on and get a paid account with one of the other sites. Be sure to research those sites to determine which one offers what you need. Whether you're a newbie starting out or an intermediate to advanced blogger, these sites give you the best opportunities for bringing traffic to your bookkeeping website.

Create Interactive Elements

Your blog may provide a place where you sound off on your thoughts and offer valuable advice, but a good tip would also be to offer some interactive elements.

Part of what makes blogs so fascinating is that they hold the possibility of developing a loyal readership. If there is nothing on your blog that people can "do" other than read, it's going to be hard to develop a relationship with your readers. If the trust and the relationship don't develop, your success with it may be hindered.

Examples of interactive elements would include a comments section and a poll section. Comments are generally included in the set up of your blog. This is where people can comment on the things you write, and communicate with you and other readers.

Polls are available as a blog "widget," and they are beneficial to have in the sidebar of your blog. You can ask a question and have visitors choose their response.

Including these interactive elements will allow you to provide readers with what they're seeking: making them loyal readers for a long time to come. You could add:

- Polls to find out when the reader is planning to find a bookkeeper

- Links to websites that a new business owner will find helpful such as local government agencies, state tax authorities, etc.

- A calendar showing upcoming important tax dates.

Optimize Your Monetization

Once your site is up and running, you'll need to make sure it's set up to make money. What this means is placing and positioning ads on your blog to increase your income. It's also important to make sure you're serving your readers with ads that interest them and are related to bookkeeping and small business topics.

Making additional money with a blog is great, but don't forget, your primary purpose in having a blog is to drive traffic to your bookkeeping website, so don't use too many ads.

Conclusion

We've covered a lot of territory in this book and I hope that you've uncovered some promotional ideas that you want to act on right away.

Don't let this information just sit on your bookshelf. Get started today by creating your marketing plan using the **"Advertising Campaign Spreadsheet"** as shown on page 15.

The sooner you get started, the sooner you'll land bookkeeping clients for your business and start making money. Nothing compares with the feeling of depositing a client's check!

I'd love to hear how you're doing. Please send me an email and let me know how your bookkeeping business is progressing. I find it very rewarding knowing that people have taken my materials and are successfully using them to earn their income from bookkeeping.

You can email me at **sylviajaumann@gmail.com**.

Sylvia Jaumann

Resources

"Most people have no idea of the giant capacity we can immediately command when we focus all of our resources on mastering a single area of our lives."

Tony Robbins

Additional Resources

Bookkeeping Associations

Canada:

The Institute of Professional Bookkeepers of Canada (IPBC) – www.ipbc.ca

United States:

The American Institute of Professional Bookkeepers (AIPB) – www.aipb.org

Australia:

The Australian Association of Professional Bookkeepers (AAPB) – www.aapb.org.au

United Kingdom:

The Institute of Certified Bookkeepers (ICB) – www.bookkeepers.org.uk/

Bookkeeping Websites

Bookkeeper List

This is a directory where you can list your bookkeeping business.

www.BookkeeperList.com

The Freelance Bookkeeper Blog

My friend Gabrielle Fontaine runs this blog and posts first-rate articles on freelance bookkeeping.

www.TheFreelanceBookkeeper.com/blog

More by the Author

Secrets to Starting & Running Your Own Bookkeeping Business

Looking for more information on starting a bookkeeping business? Find out how to set up systems to keep track of clients, how to track your billing hours, how to set up your hourly rate, and much more.

Go to **www.1stRateBooks.com** for more information.

How to Get Bookkeeping Clients Quickly - Free Resources

As mentioned throughout the book, this is where you'll find the following marketing materials to promote your bookkeeping business:

- Ad Campaign Spreadsheet
- Accountant Letter
- Ask the Bookkeeping Pro ads (in Publisher format)
- Letterhead samples (in Publisher format)
- Marketing Services Kit
- Press Release Template
- Free Reports / Ebooks

www.GetBookkeepingClients.com/gbc-resources.html

How to Get Bookkeeping Clients Quickly - Enhanced Package - $16.95

- 12 Sales Letters
- Mailing List Spreadsheet
- 20 Articles
- 12 Ezines
- 9 Day Ecourse

Go to:

www.GetBookkeepingClients.com/enhanced.html

Bookkeeper Wanted Directory

My bookkeeping resource directory, where you can list your bookkeeping business online for a small monthly fee.

www.BookkeeperWanted.net

INDEX

About the Author

Sylvia Jaumann, author of *How to Get Bookkeeping Clients Quickly: The Bookkeeping Business Marketing Guidebook* and *Secrets to Starting & Running Your Own Bookkeeping Business: Freelance Bookkeeping at Home* has been a professional bookkeeper for more than eighteen years. Years ago, Sylvia decided to go out on her own and start her own bookkeeping business as she knew that self-employed bookkeepers make more money than employed ones.

But she found the going tough for the first year as she struggled with all the requirements needed to start a bookkeeping business and make it profitable. There was literally no information on how to start a bookkeeping business available at the time, so she had a lot to learn along the way.

She ended up subcontracting for a professional bookkeeper just to make ends meet and discovered many tips and tricks to running a bookkeeping business that she didn't know before.

Sylvia took what she learned and turned it into the aforementioned books so that bookkeepers from all over the world can benefit from her experience and not struggle like she did.